This book belongs to:

Delightful Dinosaurs & Playful Prehistoric Beasts Coloring Book

Mary Lou Brown
Sandy Mahony

adventurelearningpress.com

www.ingramcontent.com/pod-product-compliance
Lightning Source LLC
Chambersburg PA
CBHW081138280526
45787CB00007B/3137
9781533306319